W9-BNY-892

N. T. WRIGHT
FOR EVERYONE
BIBLE STUDY GUIDES

1 & 2 PETER AND JUDE

9 STUDIES FOR INDIVIDUALS AND GROUPS

N. T. WRIGHT

WITH DALE AND SANDY LARSEN

IVP Connect

An imprint of InterVarsity Press
Downers Grove, Illinois

InterVarsity Press
P.O. Box 1400, Downers Grove, IL 60515-1426
World Wide Web: www.ivpress.com
E-mail: email@ivpress.com

© 2012 by Nicholas Thomas Wright

All rights reserved. No part of this book may be reproduced in any form without written permission from InterVarsity Press.

This study guide is based on and includes excerpts adapted from The Early Christian Letters for Everyone, © 2011 Nicholas Thomas Wright. All New Testament quotations, unless otherwise indicated, are taken from The Kingdom New Testament published in the United States by HarperOne and from The New Testament for Everyone published in England by SPCK; copyright © 2011 by Nicholas Thomas Wright. Used by permission of SPCK, London. All rights reserved.

InterVarsity Press® is the book-publishing division of InterVarsity Christian Fellowship/USA®, a movement of students and faculty active on campus at hundreds of universities, colleges and schools of nursing in the United States of America, and a member movement of the International Fellowship of Evangelical Students. For information about local and regional activities, write Public Relations Dept., InterVarsity Christian Fellowship/USA, 6400 Schroeder Rd., P.O. Box 7895, Madison, WI 53707-7895, or visit the IVCF website at <www.intervarsity.org>.

Cover design: Cindy Kiple
Cover image: Alexa Miller/Getty Images
Interior design: Beth Hagenberg

ISBN 978-0-8308-2197-6

Printed in the United States of America ∞

 InterVarsity Press is committed to protecting the environment and to the responsible use of natural resources. As a member of Green Press Initiative we use recycled paper whenever possible. To learn more about the Green Press Initiative, visit <www.greenpressinitiative.org>.

P   20   19   18   17   16   15   14   13   12   11   10   9   8   7   6   5   4   3   2

Y   29   28   27   26   25   24   23   22   21   20   19   18   17   16   15   14

CONTENTS

Getting the Most Out of
1 & 2 Peter and Jude

The small groups of believers must have been very concerned. Here they were, far from Jerusalem, the founding center of the church and of their faith, dispersed in the regions of Pontus, Galatia, Cappadocia, Asia and Bithynia (what is now Turkey). Did the persecution which was increasing mean that they were on the wrong road? Had they taken a false turning? Had they given their allegiance to Jesus as a false Messiah? If not, then why would these things still be happening?

What's more, weren't they in the last days? Hadn't the death and resurrection of Jesus ushered in the kingdom of God? Then why were pagans still ruling? Why was Jesus himself not on the throne? Why the delay? People were scoffing and ridiculing them. Things seemed to be going on in the world just as before with no difference, said those mocking them. So the believers wondered, Should we be listening to new teachers instead of to the gospel message we originally heard?

In response to this situation, Peter wrote two letters. As is so often the case with ancient letters (and early Christian letters are no exception), we find, at the end, just a flicker of a hint about the actual circumstances of writing. In 1 Peter 5:12-14, we read of "Silvanus" who is taking this letter to the churches in Turkey. Is this the same "Silas" we meet with Paul in Acts, or indeed the "Silvanus" mentioned by Paul as being with him when he was writing 1 and 2 Thessalonians? It may have been quite a common name. Nor can we be absolutely sure when

Peter says he is writing from "Babylon" in 5:13 that this is really code for "Rome," as in the book of Revelation. Mark, mentioned as "my son," is almost certainly the John Mark we meet in Acts, and again at the end of Colossians, Philemon and 2 Timothy.

Some people doubt that what we call 2 Peter was written by Peter himself, but several parts of it indicate that it is indeed supposed to come from him in some sense, even if he didn't physically write it himself. In 2 Peter 3:1 he notes explicitly that this is the second letter to this group of believers. We find in 2 Peter 1:13-15 that he knows his own time to die is drawing near. Jesus had warned him of this (John 21:18-19), and 2 Peter 1:14 may refer to a later word which Peter had received. It was important to be sure that his readers would be able to hold on to the truths which he had taught. The death of an apostle must not mean the decline of the apostolic faith.

Then in 2 Peter 1:16-18 we find the only time outside the first three Gospels that anyone refers to the "transfiguration," the time when Jesus was suddenly radiant with light, talking with Moses and Elijah, and when a voice from heaven proclaimed that he was indeed God's son. Here Jesus had been revealed to Peter, James and John, as they stood with him on the mount (Mark 9:2-8). This story, Peter insists, is not a "cleverly devised myth." Presumably by this stage in the early church some of the opponents of the faith were scoffing at the extraordinary tales that were going around about Jesus. Peter insists that it was the truth. He was an eyewitness not just of this but of all Jesus had said and done during their three years together.

All this is based, as much of the letters are, on Peter's awareness that the sudden dramatic events of the previous few decades—the life, death and resurrection of Jesus, the giving of the Spirit, and the rise and spread of the early Christian movement—has not been a totally new idea, starting from scratch. On the contrary. It is the fulfillment, admittedly in very surprising ways, of the age-old divine plan which the ancient prophets had glimpsed. The prophets were people who stood on the borders between heaven and earth, between our present time and God's future time. They came to know God so well (a very painful experience, as some of them discovered) that they could discern the shape of his plan: to rescue the world through the sufferings of his chosen one, his anointed, the Messiah, and then to establish the Messiah in "glory," that is, as the sovereign over the world.

Not only that, Peter's solid reassurance was based on the rest of Scripture, based on his sense of how God's purpose was always going to work out and based above all on Jesus himself. Hold on to his death and resurrection, he says. That's the sheet-anchor. He is the true Messiah, and one day will be publicly revealed as such. This is the true grace of God; stand firm in it. And—the note that we all need, especially when the going is tough: peace. Peace to you from God. Peace to you in the Messiah.

Finally, in this guide, prepared with the help of Dale and Sandy Larsen for which I am grateful, we include the letter traditionally known as Jude (though the name can also be translated as "Judah"). We are not absolutely sure who he is. He describes himself as "brother of James" which probably means James the brother of Jesus. There is a "Judah" who is mentioned among those brothers in Mark 6:3. But, since Jesus was taken from them perhaps three or more decades before, it may seem more natural to speak of himself as brother of the leader who is either still alive or else only recently dead. In any case, he calls himself "slave of Jesus"; even if he, too, was a son of Mary he would not presume to describe himself as Jesus' brother.

It's interesting, isn't it, that we tend to call him "Jude," thereby distinguishing him from two others who had the same name: Judah the patriarch, the ancestor of Jesus, and Judas Iscariot. Why have we done that? He has a royal and ancient name, and I prefer that he should keep it. So while I have retained the traditional name in the title of this guide to avoid confusion, I have used "Judah" in the text. (For more on all these letters also see my *The Early Christian Letters for Everyone* published by SPCK and Westminster John Knox, on which this guide is based. New Testament quotations in this guide are from my own translation, published as *The Kingdom New Testament* by HarperOne in the United States and published as *The New Testament for Everyone* by SPCK in England.)

Judah told his readers that he had been going to write about "the rescue in which we share"—God's rescue of us in Jesus the Messiah, the great saving acts which all Christian teachers love to celebrate. But he had to put those plans on hold, because it appeared that the church had been infiltrated with people teaching what was basically a different message altogether. And the ordinary Christians, with no long centuries of experience behind them in the church, were deeply vulnerable. If new teaching sounded exciting and fun, why not give it a try? No, says Judah: it's time to put your climbing ropes on. These rocks are dangerous and difficult. It's time to struggle hard for the faith which was once and for all given to God's people.

Both Peter and Judah note that there are tough things which must be faced. But with our new identity, and with the powerful mercy of God keeping us safe, there is such a thing as sustained and lasting growth in Christian character, faith and life. It is your privilege and birthright, as a follower of Jesus, that you should grow in grace and in the knowledge of our Lord and Savior Jesus the Messiah.

I have a sense that these letters might be a word for our times. If our desire is to bring God glory both now and in the day when his new age dawns, we could do a lot worse than to study them carefully, pray them, take them to heart and put them into practice.

SUGGESTIONS FOR INDIVIDUAL STUDY

1. As you begin each study, pray that God will speak to you through his Word.

2. Read the introduction to the study and respond to the "Open" question that follows it. This is designed to help you get into the theme of the study.

3. Read and reread the Bible passage to be studied. Each study is designed to help you consider the meaning of the passage in its context. The commentary and questions in this guide are based on my own translation of each passage found in the companion volume to this guide in the For Everyone series on the New Testament (published by SPCK and Westminster John Knox).

4. Write your answers to the questions in the spaces provided or in a personal journal. Each study includes three types of questions: observation questions, which ask about the basic facts in the passage; interpretation questions, which delve into the meaning of the passage; and application questions, which help you discover the implications of the text for growing in Christ. Writing out your responses can bring clarity and deeper understanding of yourself and of God's Word.

5. Each session features selected comments from the For Everyone series. These notes provide further biblical and cultural background and contextual information. They are designed not to answer the questions for you but to help you along as you study the Bible for yourself. For even more reflections on each passage, you may wish to have on hand a copy of the companion volume from the For Everyone series as you work through this study guide.

6. Use the guidelines in the "Pray" section to focus on God, thanking him for what you have learned and praying about the applications that have come to mind.

SUGGESTIONS FOR GROUP MEMBERS

1. Come to the study prepared. Follow the suggestions for individual study mentioned above. You will find that careful preparation will greatly enrich your time spent in group discussion.

2. Be willing to participate in the discussion. The leader of your group will not be lecturing. Instead, she or he will be asking the questions found in this guide and encouraging the members of the group to discuss what they have learned.

3. Stick to the topic being discussed. These studies focus on a particular passage of Scripture. Only rarely should you refer to other portions of the Bible or outside sources. This allows for everyone to participate on equal ground and for in-depth study.

4. Be sensitive to the other members of the group. Listen attentively when they describe what they have learned. You may be surprised

by their insights! Each question assumes a variety of answers. Many questions do not have "right" answers, particularly questions that aim at meaning or application. Instead the questions push us to explore the passage more thoroughly.

When possible, link what you say to the comments of others. Also, be affirming whenever you can. This will encourage some of the more hesitant members of the group to participate.

5. Be careful not to dominate the discussion. We are sometimes so eager to express our thoughts that we leave too little opportunity for others to respond. By all means participate! But allow others to also.

6. Expect God to teach you through the passage being discussed and through the other members of the group. Pray that you will have an enjoyable and profitable time together, but also that as a result of the study you will find ways that you can take action individually and/ or as a group.

7. It will be helpful for groups to follow a few basic guidelines. These guidelines, which you may wish to adapt to your situation, should be read at the beginning of the first session.

- Anything said in the group is considered confidential and will not be discussed outside the group unless specific permission is given to do so.

- We will provide time for each person present to talk if he or she feels comfortable doing so.

- We will talk about ourselves and our own situations, avoiding conversation about other people.

- We will listen attentively to each other.

- We will be very cautious about giving advice.

Additional suggestions for the group leader can be found at the back of the guide.

RANSOMED BY GRACE

1 Peter 1:1–2:3

If we are wise, we regularly take a car to be serviced, so that anything which is starting to go wrong can be put right. In the same way, we need to remind ourselves frequently, seriously and thoroughly who we really are. Unless we do that, the insidious messages we get from the world around (that we are who we are because of who our parents were, where we live or how much we earn) will eat away at us like rust into a car.

At the beginning of his letter to scattered Christians, Peter doesn't address these people in terms of their ancestry, their moral background, their social status, their wealth or poverty. While all those things are part of their old identity, he is sketching out the new one. It is easy to forget our basic identity as Christians, and it is therefore important to be reminded of it on a regular basis. We are people who, by the grace of God, have been chosen for a particular purpose. All Christians live a strange double life: Peter addresses his audience as *foreigners,* not because they have emigrated to where they now live but because they now have a dual citizenship. They are simultaneously inhabitants of this or that actual country or district (Pontus, Galatia or wherever), and citizens of God's new world which, as he will shortly say, is waiting to be unveiled.

OPEN

What are some ways that people try to define themselves or find their identity?

STUDY

1. *Read 1 Peter 1:1-9.* What are the various ways Peter says believers have a special identity in Christ?

2. Think through what this means. What can be the effects in our lives of embracing or failing to embrace these truths about who we are?

3. Peter says in 1:6-7 that suffering and trials benefit our faith. How does and doesn't this make sense to you?

4. What does Peter say are Christians' reasons for joy?

Through the Messiah's sacrificial death on the one hand and the indwelling of God's Spirit on the other hand, God has set people apart to be living signals of a new world. They are therefore to be "holy," both in the technical sense that God has set them apart for this purpose and in the practical sense that their actual lives have been transformed. We have become new people—a theme that Peter will shortly explore quite a bit further. A new life has come to birth within us because a new life has come to birth in the world in the resurrection from the dead of Jesus the Messiah (1:3). Becoming a Christian means that what God did for Jesus at Easter he does for you, in the very depth of your being.

5. *Read 1 Peter 1:10-21.* What was the role of the Old Testament prophets regarding the coming of the Messiah?

6. In 1:13 Peter says we should get our minds ready for action. What part does our mind have in a life of faith and obedience?

7. According to Peter in 1:13-17, what are the connections between hope and holiness?

8. Since you put faith in Christ, how have your hopes changed?

9. How can the world still squash us into the shape of the passions we had before we knew Christ (1:14)?

Suppose you go into a junk shop and find a cracked bowl, still dirty with soil and the remains of a few leaves. You spot (as the shop owner obviously hasn't) that it is a fine piece of porcelain. You buy it, take it home, clean it up and repair the crack. When it is done, you put it in a place of honor, where it holds three gorgeous ornamental eggs and shows them off to perfect effect.

Now suppose the original owner of the bowl turns up at the junk shop and asks for the bowl back to hold a few flowers. The shop owner might direct him to you; but you, perfectly properly, would say that the bowl is no longer available. Not only have you bought it, you have cleaned it inside and out and given it a new use, for which it was really suited. It would be an insult as well as an injustice to the bowl to use it to hold a few flowers.

The good news is that we are like that bowl. We have been bought back like a dirty object in a junk shop. We had all been used for all kinds of purposes other than those for which we were made. God has come into the junk shop and has paid the ultimate price for us: the precious blood of the Messiah, God's own son. Remind yourself of that, and don't let any previous owners come up and try to force you back into the use you once had.

10. *Read 1 Peter 1:22–2:3.* Most Christians struggle, at least some of the time, with having a sincere love for all their fellow believers (1:22). What reasons does Peter offer for Christians loving one another?

Peter uses another picture: that of the farmer sowing seed. This is no ordinary seed. It is the living and abiding word of God (1:23). Many Christians assume that "the word of God" simply means "the Bible," and the phrase is often used in that sense. But when Peter was writing, the New Testament as we know it didn't exist except for a few bits and pieces circulating here and there. For him "the Bible" would have meant the ancient Israelite Scriptures, the Old Testament. But Peter seems to mean more than that. When he speaks of "the word that was announced to you" (1:25), he seems to mean the message about Jesus the Messiah, about God sending him so that through his sacrificial death and his outpoured Spirit, people from every nation might be ransomed from their previous life and given a whole new life and purpose in God's service.

11. What has the seed of "the word" accomplished in the world and in your own life?

As early as the day of Pentecost, the followers of Jesus discovered that when they spoke to people about Jesus, something happened. It wasn't just that people were interested or that they decided either to go along with the message or to reject it. It was that the "word" carried an energy, a power, beyond the mere "words." When the "word" was spoken, something like a blood transfusion took place in at least some of the hearers. They found themselves gripped by it, transformed by it, rinsed out by it, given a new sense of the presence of God. Hearing "the word," they "tasted that the Lord is gracious." They had been born again.

12. Peter reminds us that there is more to salvation than initially being saved. Salvation is something we grow up in (2:2). Having tasted that the Lord is good, we should go on to crave the spiritual milk, the real stuff, not watered down. What does it mean to grow in our salvation?

PRAY

Read through 1 Peter 1:3-5 again, this time turning it into a prayer of praise for your own salvation. Ask God to show you any ways in which you are tempted to conform to the disobedience of the world. Pray that you will live in holiness, reflecting the holiness of God.

2

LIVING STONES

1 Peter 2:4-25

For gardeners, stones are simply a nuisance. They get in the way. But for a first-century Jew who knew the Scriptures, the very word *stone* carried a double promise. First, the great hope of Israel was that the true God, Yahweh, would return to Zion (Jerusalem) at last, coming back to live forever in the temple, once it had been properly rebuilt as a suitable residence for him. There was a long tradition of speaking about the temple being built on the "rock," on the "cornerstone." Find the right "stone" and you may be on the way to building the new temple, ready for God to return. Second, the word *stone* in ancient Hebrew is very like the word for *son*. Just as our word *son* has three out of the five letters of *stone*, so the Hebrew word for *son, ben,* has three out of the four letters of the word for *stone, eben*.

How do the "stone" and the "son" join up? In a famous biblical promise, much quoted in Jesus' day, God promised David that his "son" would build the temple in Jerusalem, and that this son of David would actually be the son of God himself (2 Samuel 7:12-14). The way some people, including the early Christians, were reading the prophecies of Isaiah, the chosen, precious cornerstone (1 Peter 2:6) was no longer a physical stone itself, but a human being, the coming king, upon whom Israel's God would build something quite new.

OPEN

When have you discarded something, only to discover later that you had a real need for it? What steps did you take to get back the discarded item?

STUDY

1. *Read 1 Peter 2:4-10.* Consider the original "living stone" (v. 4). What was the contrast between the true identity of that living stone and how he was misunderstood?

2. Throughout this passage what different words and phrases does Peter use to describe Christians?

3. Which descriptive word or phrase resonates the most with you, and why?

Peter wants the scattered communities around the Mediterranean to which he is writing to get it firmly in their minds that they, too, are part of this new temple. The early church was, of course, solidly Jewish. But Peter, like Paul, saw that God had brought non-Jews into this family, to share Israel's destiny with those Jews who, like Peter and the other apostles, had believed in Jesus despite the enormous shock to the system of having a crucified Messiah. To stress the point, Peter picks up in 2:10 a famous passage from Hosea 2:23.

The people who before were not a people are now God's people. The people who had not received mercy now have received mercy. This holy nation Peter mentions is not just referring to ethnic Israel but to people of all ethnicities and nations.

4. What practical effect can this reality of a multinational and multi-ethnic people of God have on our local churches?

5. *Read 1 Peter 2:11-25.* What good results can we expect from keeping up good conduct among unbelievers (vv. 11-12)?

Peter says that you have a "true life," the hidden life of your real self, the new self as described in 1:1-5 and 2:4-10. The bodily desires, if given their head, will conduct a military campaign against that true life. One of the reasons the Christian faith spread, despite persecution, is that people gradually saw that this was a new way of life, a way which nobody had ever imagined could happen. Some Christians were tempted to ignore the basic principles of right and wrong, imagining themselves to be so utterly removed from ordinary life, so superspiritual, that they were above "right and wrong" altogether. Not so, says Peter. The world needs to see that your conduct is honorable.

6. How can Christians show respect to governments and rulers even when we think they are wrong (vv. 13-17)?

7. Peter says God's people should do good and behave well in order to silence their critics. In what other concrete ways can Christians "do good" and "behave well" in order to silence their critics?

As the letter goes on, we realize that Peter is not imagining for a moment that this will be easy, or that the authorities will always and instantly respect the followers of Jesus. Far from it. The Christians will be called to suffer, to suffer greatly, to suffer unjustly—after the pattern of Jesus himself. But all that happens within this solid advice, to which the moral and social compass must swing back after whatever interruptions may occur. Christians are to respect all people. They are to love the family—in other words, to share with other Christians anything that is needed. They must always put God himself first in everything. And—they must pay respect to the emperor. Though *respect* does not mean, of course, that you agree with everything the emperor says and does.

8. How do you respond to Peter's directives for slaves (vv. 18-20)?

9. Looking at 2:21-25, how does Peter say Christ faced suffering and injustice?

10. How does the example of Christ affect your outlook on the unjust suffering you have faced or do face?

In the ancient world, more or less everything that today is done by electricity, gas and motorized engines was done by slaves. Quite a few Christians were slaves, as you might expect granted that the gospel of Jesus gives dignity and self-worth to those who believe it. Peter addresses these Christian slaves. Instead of telling them (as we might prefer) that they should rise up in revolt against their masters, he tells them to obey and to show respect, not only when the masters in question are kindly and fair-minded, but also when they are unjust.

Here, from our point of view, he sails very close to the wind. Putting up with unjust suffering looks, to us, very much like colluding with wickedness. Many a violent household, many an abusive workplace, has been able to continue acting wickedly because people have been afraid to speak out, and have kept their heads down and put up with the abuse. Blowing the whistle on such behavior can cost you your job, your home or even, in extreme cases, your life.

Peter has glimpsed a deeper truth, behind the moral quagmire. He invites followers of Jesus to inhabit Jesus' extraordinary story: to embrace it as their own, and, being healed and rescued by those events, to make them the pattern of their lives as well. The key to it all is that the crucifixion of the Messiah was the most unjust and wicked act the world had ever seen. Here was the one man who deserved nothing but praise and gratitude, and they rejected him, beat him up and killed him. As Israel's Messiah, and hence the world's true Lord, he alone could represent all the others. He alone could, completely appropriately, stand in for them.

Peter isn't simply recommending that people remain passive while suffering violence. He is urging them to realize that somehow, strangely, the sufferings of the Messiah are not only the means by which we ourselves are rescued from our own sin. They are the means, when extended through the life of his people, by which the world itself may be brought to a new place.

11. While Peter calls us to a new outlook on our own sufferings, he also calls us to do good (vv. 12, 15), which can mean relieving the suffering of others. How do you see these fitting together?

12. In what ways can you or your Christian community work to relieve suffering and injustice?

PRAY

As I was writing this, an e-mail arrived from a Christian friend who lives in a country where the Christian faith is barely tolerated and often persecuted. His livelihood has been taken away. The authorities are closing in. Receiving such a message, I feel helpless. Somehow, in prayer, and in such campaigning as we can do, those of us who read 1 Peter in comfortable freedom have a deep responsibility to help our brothers and sisters for whom the persecution of which Peter speaks is a daily reality.

Pray for persecuted Christians, both in far-off places and closer to home. Pray that they will see value in their sufferings. Bring your own sufferings to God. Entrust yourself and those you love to "the one who judges justly" (v. 23).

3

SEEK PEACE, AND FOLLOW AFTER IT

1 Peter 3

In what used to be thought of as the Christian West, particularly Europe and North America, it used to be taken for granted that we lived in a Christian country. Unless people were obviously Jews, Muslims or some other definite religion, it was assumed that everyone was more or less Christian. Now all that has been swept away, and anyone who really is Christian may well stand out. In some quarters—politics, art, the media and particularly journalism—anyone known as a Christian may well attract scorn, criticism or even discrimination. This is what it was like from the beginning. This is what it's like for probably a majority of Christians in the world today—in China, in many officially Muslim countries and so on.

It's not easy for Western Christians, faced with this shift, to unlearn old habits and learn the necessary new ones. We are not as used, as many Christians have had to be, to treading the fine line between sinking without a trace into the surrounding culture, on the one hand, and adopting a stand-offish, holier-than-thou approach on the other.

OPEN

Why do Christians tend to gravitate toward either "sinking without a trace into the surrounding culture" or "adopting a stand-offish, holier-than-thou approach" rather than being able to maintain a balance?

STUDY

1. *Read 1 Peter 3:1-7.* Consider what Peter advocates here for wives and husbands. How does it depart from the views of the dominant culture around us?

2. What are the spiritual priorities Peter highlights for wives and for husbands?

What would it be like if popular magazines reflected a quite different idea about what it means to be a woman or a man? Suppose real womanly beauty comes from the heart! Suppose what gives a married woman her full stature as a human being is something that affects her whole character, rather than something merely stuck on to the outside! Now there's a radical idea.

And suppose the way a married man can find true fulfillment is not by bullying his wife into submission, forcing her to do what he wants. Suppose the way to fulfillment is through treating the wife as an equal, even though she will, in the normal run of things, be less physically strong. Suppose, in religious terms as well as other ways, she stands on level ground with him. Now there's a radical idea.

What would it be like if Christians were to start cheerfully behaving in that different way, whether or not the magazine trade caught up with the idea? The fact that this still sounds quite drastic indicates that this is a lesson each generation has to learn.

3. *Read 1 Peter 3:8-16.* How does Peter expand his advice for married couples and apply it to Christians in general?

4. When we deal with those outside the faith, what attitudes should we carry in our hearts?

5. Why is it so difficult to not repay evil with evil but instead with blessing (v. 9)?

6. In what ways, large or small, have you experienced criticism or rejection for your faith or for doing good (vv. 13-14)?

7. What is the reason for the hope in you (v. 15)?

How does a Christian behave when surrounded by a world that doesn't understand what we're about and is potentially hostile? The answer comes in Peter's quotation from Psalm 34. *Seek peace, and follow after it.* It may be hard to find, this peace we're supposed to be looking for, but we should hunt it down as you would hunt for a favorite book that you can't find. You should follow after as you would follow a dog that runs off in a busy town. Don't expect peace to come to you when you whistle. You have to do the work. You have to learn the new habit. You have to learn it because it will be all too easy to lapse into the way many people behave.

Here is the irony: Christians are supposed to stand out as distinctive, but when we do, and are mocked or criticized for it, we are tempted to mock and criticize right back—and then we are no longer distinctive, because we are behaving just like everyone else! The new habits of heart and life are to be learned in the comparatively safe environment of the church itself (v. 8) so that they can then be practiced and applied in the wider world (v. 9 and vv. 12-16).

8. *Read 1 Peter 3:17-22.* Ordinarily we would say that it's better to suffer for doing evil than for doing good, because if you suffer for doing evil, you deserve it. Why does Peter reverse this assumption and say it is better to suffer for doing good?

9. In what ways do verses 17-22 emphasize the ultimate victory of God in Christ?

10. How is this relevant in light of the overall subject matter of 1 Peter 3?

11. What questions do verses 19-21 raise in your mind?

Many readers stumble over 1 Peter 3:19-21. We have become used to Peter warning his readers to expect suffering. Now, quite suddenly, he tells us several new things. First, after his death Jesus made a proclamation to the spirits in prison. Second, these spirits had been disobedient in the days of Noah. Third, Noah's building of an ark to rescue his family points forward to baptism. Fourth, baptism is less about washing clean and more about the appeal to God of a good conscience.

We should remind ourselves that this passage is an encouragement to people who are likely to suffer unjust treatment from the human authorities as official, legal persecution. Not only does this bring them into line with the Messiah himself, who suffered in the same way, but after his suffering *he announced God's victory over all authorities, particularly the ones in the heavenly places.* The authorities themselves, the human authorities who may be thought of as embodying spiritual authorities which stand behind them in the unseen realm, have already received notice that Jesus has overthrown their power and is now sovereign over the whole world, themselves included.

The story of Noah's ark involved people being rescued through the great flood and is a fairly obvious picture of baptism, which in Romans 6 is seen as the means of dying and rising with the Messiah. But baptism, the thing which marks out the Christian publicly from the world around, isn't just a matter of being made clean from one's former life, though it can be seen that way as well. Precisely because it functions as the boundary marker for the Christian community, it shapes the confrontation that must then take place between that community and the watching world. Baptism provides the ground (through the forgiveness of our sins through Jesus' death) for that "good conscience" (vv. 16, 21) which means that when the confrontation happens the Christian need not be ashamed.

What we need to know then, when facing trouble or persecution, is this. Jesus the Messiah has fulfilled the hope of Israel by defeating all the spiritual powers in the world, the ones who were responsible for wickedness and corruption from ancient times. It may not look like it to the little Christian communities facing the possibility of suffering, but their baptism places them alongside the Messiah in his victory. They must hold their heads up, keep their consciences clear and trust that his victory will be played out in the world to which they are bearing witness.

12. How does this affect your understanding of the significance of baptism for you?

13. What encouragement do you draw from Peter's assurance that all authorities and powers are subject to Christ (v. 22)?

PRAY

Reread 1 Peter 3:15-16 and pray that this will be consistently true in your everyday life.

If you are married or contemplating marriage, pray that your marriage will reflect the Christlike picture of 1 Peter 3:1-7.

No matter what your marital status, pray that your relationships will display the spirit of 1 Peter 3:8-9.

4

TRANSFORMED LIVING

1 Peter 4

Sometimes someone who has had a potentially fatal stroke or heart attack makes a remarkable recovery. In such cases people often say that they have rethought their whole lives, and now realize much more clearly what matters and what doesn't. In the same way, someone who has suffered for the gospel may attain a new kind of clarity. They see more sharply the kind of world that sin produces, and they know that they are done with it. And they see, far more gloriously, that God's will is the only thing worth following. It is not pleasant to be persecuted. But if, when it happens, you can see it as a road sign telling you that you are on the right path, that may make all the difference. Like the Messiah, we must put on the mental armor that will make us strong to face the suffering which we may have to face.

OPEN

When have you had a renewed sense of clarity and purpose in following Christ? How was suffering involved in that realization?

STUDY

1. *Read 1 Peter 4:1-11.* Why are Christians to turn away from the behaviors and attitudes of their former lives (vv. 1-4)?

2. Perhaps even in your pre-Christian days, you never engaged in the sort of activities Peter describes in verse 3. Even if you were outwardly moral then, how specifically has Christ rearranged your priorities and values?

Peter is saying that pagan ways have had quite enough of your time already. Why should they have any more? Nothing is to be gained from licentious and lawless behavior. It merely wastes the time you could be growing as a human being, discovering more about how God's love can transform your life and that of those around you. After all, that is what you are here for (vv. 8-11). There is plenty to occupy any Christian in reflecting God's love to others, in using to God's glory the gifts we have been given.

3. Have you faced a situation like the one in verse 4? If so, how did you deal with it?

In the middle of this quite clear line of thought we have a genuinely puzzling passage in verse 6. When he here (4:6) says that the gospel was preached even to the dead, are these the spirits in prison of 3:19? The best answer is, No, they are not. Here, as there, the overall context is the vital thing. Peter, as ever, is encouraging those facing hostility because of their following the Messiah. He says it will all be sorted out at the judgment. At death, to the pagan, it may look as though the

Christians have lost the struggle. But these Christians, now dead, had already received the powerful word of the gospel which was preached to them during their lifetime. Now, by God's Spirit, they are alive in God's presence, awaiting the resurrection which is yet to come.

4. In 4:7 Peter says that the end of all things is upon us. What did he mean? Did he mean that the space-time universe was about to come to a shuddering halt any minute? That would hardly be a vindication of the God who made it and loved it, nor, two thousand years later, would it seem a very accurate prophecy. Rather for Peter as for the whole of early Christianity, what had happened in Jesus' death and resurrection was the ushering in of a whole new world. So he means that this is therefore the beginning of the end of life as we know it. God has already started, in Jesus, the process of the final age in which there will be cosmic renewal. The sign and foretaste of this is the renewal of human lives through sharing Jesus' death and resurrection.

In this light, what then is the connection between this "end of all things" (v. 7) and our behavior now (vv. 7-11)?

5. Looking at 4:7 again, how are clear thinking, self-discipline and prayer connected?

6. Which of these instructions in 4:7-11 could you put into practice this week, and how?

7. In verse 8 Peter quotes from Proverbs 10:12 the famous saying that "love covers a multitude of sins." He doesn't mean that love is a cover-

up operation, hiding things we'd rather not face. Rather, the gift of love we are invited to offer one another minute by minute, day by day, actually *transforms* situations, so that the multitude of sins which were there before are taken out of the equation. They are forgiven!

How has love helped you deal with other people's sins (v. 8)?

8. *Read 1 Peter 4:12-19.* It must have come as a great surprise to the early Christians to discover that even though the Messiah had been raised from the dead, there was still a period of time in which intense suffering would occur to his people.

   We may experience the same surprise today, but why should suffering *not* surprise us?

9. It might also seem strange to us, as it likely seemed to Peter's first readers, to think of being insulted because of the name of Christ as a blessing (v. 14). So Peter gives the example of criminals suffering because of their wrongdoing (v. 15). In that case, their suffering highlights for all to see the shame of what they've done and who they are.

   How does this contrast with what suffering means as a Christian (v. 16)?

10. Judgment will begin, not with the obviously wicked, but with God's own household (v. 17). From God's perspective, the holiest, most loving person is still someone who needs to be rescued. That person is still so weighed down with sin that without the grace and mercy

shown through Jesus, the rescue would not happen. This alarming reflection is not meant to produce panic, but rather gratitude.

What comfort and assurance can you draw from verses 17-18?

11. In what areas of your life do you have difficulty trusting the faithful Creator by doing what is good (v. 19)?

"Doing good" (v. 19) is much more positive than rule keeping, keeping your nose clean, not getting into trouble. It means bringing fresh goodness, fresh love, fresh kindness, fresh wisdom into the community, into the family, to the people we meet on the street. When we do this, we are not saying, "Look at me, aren't I being good?" We are saying to God, "I trust you; this is what you have called me to do; this is what I am doing with the life you've given me; even though I am facing suffering, I will continue to be this sort of a person, to your glory."

12. What would be a clear, practical way in which you could show you entrust your life to the faithful Creator by doing what is good?

PRAY

Pray that you will be able to keep firm in your love for others despite their shortcomings, because "love covers a multitude of sins" (v. 8).

Pray that your attitude in suffering will not be surprise or resentment but trust in God and forgiveness toward others. If you are being mistreated for the name of Christ, ask God to help you see it as a blessing and give you profound joy that you are sharing the sufferings of the Messiah (v. 13).

STAND FIRM

1 Peter 5

From time to time the television or the newspapers tell us that there is a crisis of leadership. What that means, often enough, is that the media disapprove of the political leaders we happen to have at the moment. Even without that rather cynical observation, I find myself anxious about discussion of leadership in a vacuum. What I find is that anything worth calling leadership happens, often without people thinking about it as such, when someone is so energetically and productively involved in whatever it is (whether making music, running a business, organizing a shop or heading up a government department) that they communicate that energy and productivity, that enthusiasm and effectiveness, to those around them. Leadership, in other words, is a bit like friendship: it's something that happens best when you're not thinking about it but instead about whatever it is that you're actually doing together.

OPEN

Who are some good leaders you have worked with? What made those people good leaders?

STUDY

1. *Read 1 Peter 5:1-7.* Peter appeals to the elders as a fellow elder. The word translated "elder" means "senior," both in the sense of status within the community and in the sense of older in years, and the two often go together, of course.

    What attitudes does Peter say should be in the heart of an elder in the church?

    What attitudes should *not* be there?

2. Peter admonishes the shepherds not to "lord it over those for whom [they] are responsible, but rather be an example to the flock" (v. 3). What does it look like when leaders "lord it over" others or are overriding?

3. Why is it so common for leaders to act in this way instead of serving?

4. Why does an attitude of service produce better care for the flock than bossing or nagging?

5. How was Jesus, the Chief Shepherd, an example of humility and leadership that served the flock rather than domineered over them (v. 4)?

What Peter is describing here is not *leaders* but *shepherds*. In a rural economy, it's hardly surprising that this is one of the standard images for the way in which either God himself, or the anointed king, is to look after the "sheep." The best shepherds aren't thinking *How can I be a shepherd?* but *How can I best look after these sheep?* The focus of the good shepherd is not only on his or her own qualities but on the needs of, and potential dangers for, those they are looking after.

6. Consider what leadership or shepherding responsibilities you have. What's one way you can apply what Peter says to your situation? (If you don't think you have any particular such duties, what can you do now to prepare yourself to be the kind of leader Peter commends?)

I recently visited a large college which trains army officers. To my surprise and delight, at almost every turn I met the college's motto: "Serve to Lead." This isn't an empty slogan. They mean it, model it and teach it. Unless an officer is *serving* the soldiers in the unit—thinking about them as people, getting to know who they are, what they are afraid of, what makes them give of their best, and looking after them in those and all other ways—they will not be able to *lead* them in any difficult or dangerous situations.

7. How does Peter connect humility and hope (vv. 5-6)?

8. What anxieties is the Lord calling you to throw fully onto him (v. 7)?

9. *Read 1 Peter 5:8-14.* How do your ideas of the devil match up with Peter's picture of the devil (vv. 8-9)?

As C. S. Lewis said when writing about his world-famous book *The Screwtape Letters*, consisting of letters from a senior devil to a junior one on how to tempt people, some people dismiss the idea of a devil by thinking of a ridiculous little person with horns and hooves wearing red tights. They can't believe in a creature like that, so they decide they can't believe in the devil. Other people become so fascinated with the devil that they can think of little else, and suppose that every ordinary problem in life, or difficulty in someone else's personality, is due to direct devilish intervention. Lewis steers a wise path between these two extremes, and so should we.

10. Peter notes in verse 9 that in his day fellow Christians around the world were suffering social, economic and political pressure—sometimes punctuated by violence. And this continues to be true today. What persecution of Christians are you aware of, or, if you aren't, what can you do this week to learn more?

For most of the time in this letter we have been aware of persecution coming from the surrounding non-Christian culture. How easy it would have been, as it still is, for the Christians then to demonize their visible, human opponents, to regard them as the real source of the problem. But even your fiercest human persecutors are not in fact the real enemy. There is a real enemy, and he will be using them.

But if you resist him, staying resolute in faith and remembering that you are holding your bit of the line while your Christian brothers and sisters across the world are holding theirs, you will find that courteous and civil behavior, acting with respect and gentleness, will again and again win an answering respect from outsiders, even if they still don't understand what makes you tick.

11. Much of 1 Peter is about suffering. On what basis can Peter end his letter with the assurance of peace (v. 14)?

12. To what circumstances and relationships in your life does the entire letter of 1 Peter speak most immediately?

PRAY

As you pray, consciously throw all your care upon him, because he cares about you (v. 7).

Consider any roles in which you exercise leadership, whether at work, in the church, in your family or in your community, and pray that you will be a godly shepherd of the people he has entrusted into your care.

Pray for strength and patience to undergo suffering for Christ, whatever form it is taking in your life. Pray specifically for fellow Christians around the world who face suffering, knowing that Christ has triumphed over the ultimate enemies of death and the devil.

6

CONFIRMING YOUR CALL

2 Peter 1

My grandson, aged one-and-a-half, was taken the other day into a big toy shop. From floor to ceiling, from one end of the shop to the other, and all over the tables and stands in the middle of the shop, there were so many exciting things to see that he didn't know where to start. He looked quickly this way and that, then around, then up and down. He was in happy shock at this overload of delight. All he could say—one of his few words, but most expressive—was *"Wow!"*

That's a bit how I feel on reading quickly through the beginning of the letter we call 2 Peter. Every sentence, every word almost, glitters and flashes. Every idea beckons and says, "Look at me! This is fascinating!" And it is. But if we are to make a start, it will be good to see the big picture within which all this cluster of exciting and challenging ideas means what it means. The big picture is *what God wants for his people*.

OPEN

When you see the phrase "what God wants for his people," what comes to your mind?

STUDY

1. *Read 2 Peter 1:1-11.* As you read through Peter's inventory of what
   God has provided for us, for which of these blessings are you most
   grateful and why?

2. Peter says we are given the promises "so that [we] may run away from
   the corruption of lust that is in the world, and may become partakers
   of the divine nature" (v. 4). The word for "run away from" is sometimes
   translated "shun," as though merely pushing these things away were
   enough, like refusing a second helping of food. Peter means something closer to what Joseph did when Potiphar's wife tried to seduce
   him (Genesis 39). She made a grab at him, but he *ran away.* Running
   away from the lusts of the flesh isn't a negative thing, despite what
   people will frantically tell you today. Lust is a drug. Like all drugs it
   demands more and more but gives less and less. It turns people into
   shadows of real human beings. Like shady financial dealings, it cor-
   rupts; it does to the moral fiber what cancer does to physical cells.
   Peter urges his readers to go in the opposite direction.

   Lust is often used for inappropriate sexual desire, but *lust* can be a
   consuming desire for anything which God does not desire for us.
   What desires put you in conflict with God's will?

3. What are practical ways to run away from that desire?

4. Peter says we have these blessings so that we "may become partakers of the divine nature" (v. 4). If we say that the Holy Spirit is fully divine, and if we say that the Holy Spirit comes to live within us and transform us from within, this is essentially saying that the divine nature is already dwelling within us, leading us forward until we are suffused with God's own presence and power.

    What difference does this make to you as you pursue life and godliness?

5. As we look at verses 5-7, we could think this is about "me making myself good enough for God," which can then lead to pride or arrogance ("See what a fine Christian I've become!"). The surrounding verses indicate that Peter has something else in mind. God has already given us everything we need for such a life of godliness. Of course, all these take thought; all these take effort. They don't happen by accident. You have to want to do them; you have to choose to do them. But when you do, and pray for God's grace, promises and power to help, you will be coming to know Jesus the Messiah.

    Think of one of the qualities mentioned in verses 5-7. In what practical ways might the Holy Spirit grow that in your Christian community?

6. How do verses 5-9 challenge you concerning the times when you feel you are wasting your time, or failing to bear fruit (v. 8)?

7. Peter urges his readers to confirm God's call and choice (v. 10). He doesn't mean that they can make *God* more sure of it; rather, they can make *themselves* more sure.

    When in your growth as a Christian have you had a new sense of certainty that you were chosen by God?

8. *Read 2 Peter 1:12-21.* Peter intends to keep reminding his readers of what they already know (v. 12). Why do we need to be reminded about the truths of the gospel?

9. Why does Peter feel such urgency in what he writes (vv. 13-15)?

10. How does Peter confirm the fact that he and the other apostles were not following cleverly devised myths in what they taught (vv. 16-17)?

11. How do the Old Testament prophets fit into the gospel that Peter preached and that we believe today (vv. 19-21)?

Second Peter 1:16-18 is the only time outside the first three Gospels that anyone refers to the transfiguration—the time when Jesus was suddenly radiant with light, talking with Moses and Elijah, and when a voice from heaven proclaimed that he was God's Son (for example, Mark 9:2-13). Presumably by this stage in the early church some of the opponents of the faith were scoffing at the extraordinary tales that were going around about Jesus. Peter insists that it was the truth.

The result of this eyewitness testimony is that the apostles could look back on the entire world of biblical prophecy represented by Moses and Elijah—that great, untidy, all-over-the-place story which functioned all through as a set of signposts pointing forward to what was to come—and could see that in retrospect it all made sense.

12. How is Jesus "a lamp shining in a dark place" (v. 19) for the world?

Like all other early Christians, Peter holds firm to two things: the ancient Scriptures and the newly revealed Son of God. Until we see *him,* we don't understand where *they* were going. Until we understand *them,* we don't see the point of who *he* was and what he did. We need to hold on to both until the morning star shines in our hearts, and then, through us, shines out into the world.

PRAY

Thank God for the promises of verses 2-4. Think about the qualities in verses 5-7. Which ones do you feel you lack? Pray for the Holy Spirit to develop those qualities in you.

Pray that you will be continually reminded of the gospel, as Peter urgently wishes to remind his readers.

NOTE ON 2 PETER 1:19-21

Peter is addressing a new situation that had emerged, for which no ancient Jew had, as it were, a road map. Everything had been straining forward to the day when God's glory would be revealed, the temple would be rebuilt and the Messiah would appear to save his people. Well, that had happened, so the early Christians believed, even though it didn't look the way they had thought it would: the coming of Jesus simply *was* the fulfillment of all those aspirations. His resurrection—and, indeed, his transfiguration—proved it. But nobody had ever imagined that there would then be a further time-lag *between* the time of the Messiah's appearance and the time of the final end, the final dawning of the great day. There were no speculations about what such an interim period might be like, or even why such a period should exist.

So Peter, like the other apostles, went to work to explain, from the Scriptures, why such a delay was happening and what one should be doing in the meantime. Christians from that day to this are in the position he outlines in verse 19: Jesus, his coming, transfiguration, death and resurrection have confirmed the prophetic words of Scripture, and we hold on to these, like people clinging to a bright lamp through the darkest time of the night, until the day when Jesus reappears at last as the morning star, ready to usher in God's final great day.

But now another possible objection rears its head. Supposing this way of reading Scripture is all a Christian invention? Supposing the Bible never meant all that in the first place? Peter has a firm word for such suggestions (vv. 20 and 21). It isn't a matter of private interpretation. It isn't up to us—because Scripture itself didn't come about in the first place by individuals simply deciding to write this or that. Yes, the Bible contains a remarkably wide range of material, from poetry and history to prophecy and strange symbolic revelations. But behind the different genres, and the different authors, was the divine inspiration, not bypassing the human minds, personalities and situations in question but working through them to breathe God's Word through human words. The point is that, for us looking back, Jesus himself stands there as the fulfillment of it all.

7

FALSE PROPHETS

2 Peter 2

A year or two ago I was invited to dinner with some friends who had also invited a judge. I don't often meet senior members of the legal profession, and I was intrigued to hear what he might say about his work. My anticipation turned to shock when he told me what he'd been doing that day . . . and the day before, and the day before that. His world, he explained, was very far from the glamorous vision you see in the TV dramas. Most of what a judge has to deal with is a sad and sordid procession of people whose lives have become hopelessly murky and muddled—in and out of different relationships, in and out of debt and financial problems, in and out of jail. Everyone who goes that route drags other people down with them. That brings its own trail of personal bitterness, mutual accusations, fault-finding, self-justifying—and sometimes then self-hatred, self-harm and even suicide. It's a horrible, dark world, said the judge; and now, since he was off duty, could we please talk about something more pleasant? Had I listened to any good music recently?

This passage from 2 Peter is a bit like that judge's catalog of sad and sordid behavior. Peter is doing his best to warn his readers about the dangers they face. It isn't simply a matter of people who are basically all right but get one or two points wrong. There are seriously dangerous people out there, Peter says, and you have to learn to recognize them.

OPEN

When have you, or someone you know, been deceived or misled by someone who appeared to be a sincere Christian? Why wasn't the person's deception obvious at first? What was the outcome?

STUDY

1. *Read 2 Peter 2:1-10.* The devastating thing about false prophets and teachers is that they sound all too plausible. When you listen to them, your first impression is, "Yes: this is good; this is what we need to hear. It may not be quite what I expected, but I like the sound of it." So Peter puts up a sign which says, "Danger this way!"

   According to Peter, what are the telltale marks of false teachers (vv. 1-3)?

2. What are current examples of false teachers who match these characteristics?

3. If the marks of false teachers are so obviously repellent, why do you think Christians sometimes fall for them?

4. The stories in verses 4-8 are drawn from the early chapters of Genesis, and they reflect subsequent Jewish traditions in which the plots and the characters are developed a bit further. Peter's readers would be more familiar with these stories than we are. Notice that the wickedness which God judges is not so much offbeat teaching about theoretical matters, but the practices which give the game away: sin, ungodliness, and shameful and unprincipled behavior. Nonetheless, Peter doesn't simply highlight the dangers of false teaching and behavior and the fact that God will bring judgment upon such things. He is more encouraging than that.

How does this passage also hold out hope for the genuine believer?

5. *Read 2 Peter 2:10-22.* It's a pity we today don't reflect more on angels, on what they are and what they do. They turn up all over the place, of course—on calendars, on Christmas trees, on greeting cards and so on. We rather like the idea of angels, but we have made them cozy and domestic. They are safe like that. We don't need to take them seriously. But in fact God's creation is peopled with all kinds of beings, and it seems that the angels have a hand in running the world, so that people who want to cast off authority begin by rubbishing the God-given invisible powers that stand behind human authorities.

How does Peter contrast false teachers with angels (vv. 10-11)?

6. How does Peter compare false teachers with animals (vv. 12-13)?

Peter says in verses 15-16 that it's like the time when the strange prophet Balaam was doing his best to earn money from Israel's enemies by cursing Israel, until his own donkey spoke up and rebuked him (Numbers 22). There is a sense about such people that they are indeed plugged into a kind of spiritual power, but that they are using it for their own gain. And, notoriously, when Balaam found he couldn't curse the Israelites to earn his money from the pagan king, he advised him to try a different tack. Send in seductive women, who will lead God's people into immorality and from there into idolatry (Numbers 31:15-16). That will do the trick. It still works today.

7. What impulses and desires control false teachers (vv. 13-18)?

8. The false teachers promise their followers freedom. Why is their promise deceitful (vv. 19-22)?

9. What parallel situations do you see today in which, under the banner of freedom, people are actually enslaved?

10. How have you experienced true freedom in Christ?

11. Peter's language throughout this passage is harsh. Why do you think he uses such strong imagery for false teachers?

We ought to read this passage not with a self-righteous pride ("Oh, yes, look at those wicked people! Not at all like us!") but with appropriate sorrow and fear. These tendencies are present in all of us. The point of self-control is to keep them back, to crucify wrong desires and grow right ones in their place.

PRAY

Ask God for wisdom to discern false teachers from true messengers of the gospel. Thank God for the freedom you have found in Christ. Pray for people you know who are misled, that they will see and accept the truth.

8

GOD'S PATIENCE:
OUR OPPORTUNITY

2 Peter 3

In older Bible versions, 2 Peter 3:1-10 ends with the warning that "the earth and all the works on it *will be burned up*." A cosmic destruction: the end of the physical world! Is that really what Peter wrote? If so, it's the only place in the whole of early Christian literature where such an idea is found. But in some early manuscripts of the New Testament, including two of the very best, the word for "will be burned up" isn't there. Instead there is a word which means "will be found" or "will be discovered" or "will be disclosed." Perhaps "will be found out" is another way of getting at the meaning. What I believe has happened is this. Several early scribes, faced with "will be found," thought to themselves, *That can't be right! It makes no sense! Surely Peter meant "will be burnt up."* And so the change was made.

What will happen, as many early Christian teachers said, is that some sort of "fire," literal or metaphorical, will come upon the whole earth, not to destroy, but to test everything out, and to purify it by burning up everything that doesn't meet the test. If we imagine that God wants simply to burn up the present world entirely, leaving us as disembodied souls in some kind of timeless "eternity," then why should we worry about what we do here and now? Why not just enjoy life as best we can and wait for whatever is coming next? But if God intends to *renew* the heavens and the earth as Isaiah promised (Isaiah 65:17; 66:22), then what we do in the present time matters. It matters for us, and it matters for God's world as a whole.

OPEN

When you think of Christ's second coming, what images come to your mind? What are the sources of those images?

STUDY

1. *Read 2 Peter 3:1-10.* What is Peter's purpose for writing this portion of his letter (vv. 1-2)?

2. How will scoffers call God's purposes into question (vv. 3-4)?

3. Do the questions of verse 4 ever rise in your own mind as well? If so, how do you deal with them?

4. How do the scoffers misunderstand the purposes of God (vv. 3-9)?

5. What difference does it make to our daily Christian life if we believe
    that the world we live in will be utterly destroyed or if we believe
    that this earth will be renewed by God?

Peter is clear that fire will come. But fire does not only destroy. It
can also purify, revealing the essence of a metal once everything
extraneous is removed. That is the sense Peter has here. The day
will come and all will be revealed. All will be judged with fire. That
is the promise which Peter reemphasizes here over against those
who said that the whole thing must be a mistake since Jesus had not
returned. Many in our own day have added their voices to those of
the "deceivers" of verse 3.

The misunderstanding, both ancient and modern, seems to have
come about partly because "at any time" could of course mean "therefore perhaps today or tomorrow," and partly because there really
were some things which Jesus did say (in Mark 13 and elsewhere)
would happen within a generation. But those events concerned the
destruction of Jerusalem and the temple, which did indeed happen
within a generation of Jesus' day (A.D. 70, to be precise). But Peter
warns, as Jewish teachers had done before him and would do again,
that God doesn't work on our timescales. Psalm 90:4 put it well: a
thousand years in God's sight are like a single day, and vice versa.
We can't box God in to our chronology.

What appears to us as God's delay is in fact God's moment of
fresh vocation. There are tasks to do in the meantime. But that takes
us into the next, and final, section of the letter.

6. *Read 2 Peter 3:11-18.* Knowing that the day of the Lord is coming,
    what affect should this have on our character (vv. 11-14)?

7. How does Peter comment on the apostle Paul (vv. 15-16)?

8. What opportunities does God's patience allow us (vv. 15-18)?

9. What do you have trouble waiting for?

10. How does the concept of the patience of God speak to your own struggles to be patient?

We should regard anything that looks to us like delay as an indication, not that we have to be patient with God, but that God is having to be patient with us. If God were to foreclose on the world and on ourselves straight away, what would happen? God's patience is our opportunity. It is our chance to work on the holy, godly lives we ought to be living. It is our chance, too, to spread the gospel in the world. Since we know that the day is coming, the day when new heavens and new earth will emerge, filled to the brim with God's wonderful justice, his glorious setting-right of all things, we should be working toward that already, here and now.

11. How do verses 17-18 act as a summary of the whole letter?

PRAY

If you are sure that the day of the Lord is coming, then pray about what you should be doing in the meantime. Get specific with God. Ask him to show you what he desires of you. Ask him to confirm where you are occupied with the right things.

Thank God for his patience with you and with the entire world. Submit your anxieties to him and pray for his gift of patience as you wait for him to work.

NOTE ON 2 PETER 3:15-16

By the time this letter was written, Paul's letters had already been circulating for some while in many of the churches, both in Turkey and Greece (where all of Paul's letters except Romans were addressed), and possibly further afield as well. Many early Christians were energetic travelers, and there is every indication that letters, Gospels and so on were copied, taken from place to place and studied. What Peter is saying here fits closely with a theme which, though not all readers of Paul now realize it, is in fact very important in his writings as well. For Paul, "God's kindness is meant to bring you to repentance" (Romans 2:4).

9

CONTEND FOR THE FAITH

Jude

W e are not absolutely sure, as mentioned at the beginning of this guide, of the identity of the writer we call "Jude" but which can also be translated as "Judah." He describes himself as "brother of James," which probably means James the brother of Jesus. There is a "Judah" mentioned among those brothers in Mark 6:3. We tend to call the writer "Jude," distinguishing him from two others who had the same name: Judah the patriarch and ancestor of Jesus, and Judas Iscariot. Why have we done that? He has a royal and ancient name, and so, though I have retained the traditional name in the title to avoid confusion, I've used "Judah" in the text.

Judah is clear and explicit about the twin dangers the church now faces—dangers which we can hardly hear about without realizing that this letter is very contemporary. People are transforming God's grace into licentiousness and denying the one and only Master, our Lord Jesus the Messiah (v. 4). Find people today who say that God loves everyone exactly as they are, so everyone must stay exactly as they are, doing all the things they want to do, because God is so full of generosity that obviously he wants them to do that; find such people, and you've found those of whom Judah is writing. Find people today who say that Jesus is one religious teacher among others, one way of salvation among others, that there might well be a variety of paths up the mountain of which Jesus' path is only one, that it's important not to make exclusive claims or we'll become arrogant; find such people, and you've found those of whom Judah is writing.

OPEN

What is attractive (and dangerous) about the idea that God loves all people exactly as they are, and they don't need to change?

What is attractive (and dangerous) about the idea that Jesus is only one way of salvation among others, one of many paths up the mountain?

STUDY

1. *Read verses 1-4.* What tone does Judah set at the beginning of his letter as he addresses the recipients (vv. 1-2)?

2. How does his tone change in verses 3-4, and why?

Even in his opening greeting Judah speaks of Jesus the Messiah keeping his people safe (v. 1). That is among the great truths of Jesus' present ministry, interceding for his people before the Father (see Romans 8:34). But what God loves to do, he loves to do *through others*, calling and equipping people to take his work forward. The way Jesus guards his people is, not least, by prayerful and accredited teachers encouraging them, warning them, sketching for them the bigger picture within which they can make sense of the puzzling things that are happening to them. That is what Judah is doing in his letter. He says that the very heart of Christian faith and practice is under direct attack. Unless those who are grasped by the truth of the gospel do their best to maintain it, those who are heading in another direction are going to take a lot of people with them.

3. If someone asked you, "What is the greatest danger facing the church today?"—referring to the church in your own area of the world—how would you respond?

4. *Read verses 5-16.* Judah uses many comparisons and powerful images in rapid succession, saying that the false teachers Judah's readers are facing are like those described in these stories. (See the note at the end of this study for a summary of these.)

Which stories strike you as the most disturbing, and why?

5. Judah's comparisons in verses 5-11 have in common the theme of *rebellion against authority.* What is destructive about such rebellion, whether against God himself or against human authorities instituted by God?

6. Consider the imagery of verses 12-13. How do these images reinforce the negative consequences of rebellion?

7. *Read verses 17-25.* Again the writer's tone changes. How would you describe his mood throughout this concluding section of the letter?

8. Judah does not say, "Take up the weapons and fight these false teachers on their own ground." Instead, what does he call for in verses 20-21?

9. How would following these instructions be an appropriate and effective response to those who are divisive, and who twist God's grace and deny Christ?

10. We are to have one attitude toward false teachers. But in verses 22-23 Judah recommends a different approach to the followers of these people. Who comes to your mind, and what can you do to obey Judah's directives here?

11. Judah has written his letter to warn believers of the threat of severe danger. His letter could have caused them much anxiety. How would verses 24-25 counteract their fear?

Many translations put verse 24 more negatively, "to keep you from falling." The word Judah uses is more positive, "to keep you un-stumbling." The image is of someone walking along who might have tripped and fallen, but has not done so. That is what we should pray for, and that is what we should praise God for when it happens.

Judah then gathers the whole thing up in one of the all-time classic bursts of Christian praise, praise which wells up when the Holy Spirit has flooded the heart with the knowledge of God in Jesus and of the rescue which he has accomplished. "To the one and only God, our savior through Jesus the Messiah our Lord, be glory, majesty, power and authority before all the ages, and now, and to all the ages to come. Amen." If the book of Revelation had not been written, this last verse would not have been a bad way to conclude the whole New Testament.

PRAY

"Pray in the Holy Spirit" (v. 20). One of the most important works of the Spirit is to call out prayer from the depth of our hearts, even if (as in this letter) it is a prayer of lament on the one hand and a prayer for protection on the other. It is God's lament we share as we look in sorrow at human wickedness and arrogance invading the church. It is God's protecting power and love we draw down as we pray by his Spirit in the midst of turmoil.

Use verses 20-21 to pray for yourselves. Use verses 22-23 to pray for others who are swayed by false teachers.

Conclude your time of prayer by using verses 24-25 to praise the One who, even in the midst of danger, can keep you and your fellow believers *unstumbling*.

NOTE ON VERSES 5-16

A quick review of the many biblical allusions:

- Verse 5 begins by mentioning that many Israelites whom God rescued from Egypt died before they got to the Promised Land because of their unbelief (Numbers 14:26-38).

- Verse 6 reminds us of the punishment of angels who would not obey God, which is also referenced in 2 Peter 2:4.

- Verse 7 recalls the story of Sodom and Gomorrah, which were obliterated for their sin (Genesis 19).

- Verses 8-9 reference Satan and Michael as found in Zechariah 3 and developed later in other literature outside the Bible.

- Verse 11 mentions first Cain, who was banished by God after he killed his brother Abel following God's refusal to accept Cain's offering (Genesis 4:1-16); second, Balaam, who sought to make money by cursing Israel on behalf of its enemies (Numbers 22–24); and third, how Korah led a rebellion against Moses during the forty years in the wilderness, with all the rebels dying in an earthquake (Numbers 16:1-35).

- Verse 14 quotes a Jewish text well known at the time, which puts into the mouth of the ancient figure Enoch all kinds of prophecies, including this one. Here, as in verse 9, Judah echoes Zechariah, this time 14:5: The Lord is coming with his holy ones.

NOTE ON VERSES 12-13

The false teachers are overthrowing or ignoring the proper structures of authority, and the result is moral chaos and pollution, signaled by a list of similes: waterless clouds, fruitless trees, splashing waves, wandering stars. These all appear to promise something but don't deliver it: no rain from the clouds, no fruit from the trees, no safe passage on the stormy sea, no regular movement of stars across the sky. The teachers appear to offer a way of life which is exciting, different and liberating; but the only thing they achieve is shame and darkness.

GUIDELINES FOR LEADERS

My grace is sufficient for you.
(2 Corinthians 12:9)

If leading a small group is something new for you, don't worry. These sessions are designed to flow naturally and be led easily. You may even find that the studies seem to lead themselves!

This study guide is flexible. You can use it with a variety of groups—students, professionals, coworkers, friends, neighborhood or church groups. Each study takes forty-five to sixty minutes in a group setting.

You don't need to be an expert on the Bible or a trained teacher to lead a small group. These guides are designed to facilitate a group's discussion, not a leader's presentation. Guiding group members to discover together what the Bible has to say and to listen together for God's guidance will help them remember much more than a lecture would.

There are some important facts to know about group dynamics and encouraging discussion. The suggestions listed below should equip you to effectively and enjoyably fulfill your role as leader.

PREPARING FOR THE STUDY

1. Ask God to help you understand and apply the passage in your own life. Unless this happens, you will not be prepared to lead others. Pray too for the various members of the group. Ask God to open your hearts to the message of his Word and motivate you to action.

2. Read the introduction to the entire guide to get an overview of the topics that will be explored.

3. As you begin each study, read and reread the assigned Bible passage to familiarize yourself with it. This study guide is based on the For Everyone series on the New Testament (published by SPCK and Westminster John Knox). It will help you and the group if you have on hand a copy of the companion volume from the For Everyone series both for the translation of the passage found there and for further insight into the passage.

4. Carefully work through each question in the study. Spend time in meditation and reflection as you consider how to respond.

5. Write your thoughts and responses in the space provided in the study guide. This will help you to express your understanding of the passage clearly.

6. It may help to have a Bible dictionary handy. Use it to look up any unfamiliar words, names or places. The glossary at the end of each New Testament for Everyone commentary may likewise be helpful for keeping discussion moving.

7. Reflect seriously on how you need to apply the Scripture to your life. Remember that the group members will follow your lead in responding to the studies. They will not go any deeper than you do.

LEADING THE STUDY

1. At the beginning of your first time together, explain that these studies are meant to be discussions, not lectures. Encourage the members of the group to participate. However, do not put pressure on those who may be hesitant to speak—especially during the first few sessions.

2. Be sure that everyone in your group has a study guide. Encourage the group to prepare beforehand for each discussion by reading the introduction to the guide and by working through the questions in each study.

3. Begin each study on time. Open with prayer, asking God to help the group to understand and apply the passage.

4. Have a group member read aloud the introduction at the beginning of the discussion.

5. Discuss the "Open" question before the Bible passage is read. The "Open" question introduces the theme of the study and helps group members to begin to open up, and can reveal where our thoughts and feelings need to be transformed by Scripture. Reading the passage first will tend to color the honest reactions people would otherwise give—because they are, of course, supposed to think the way the Bible does. Encourage as many members as possible to respond to the "Open" question, and be ready to get the discussion going with your own response.

6. Have a group member read aloud the passage to be studied as indicated in the guide.

7. The study questions are designed to be read aloud just as they are written. You may, however, prefer to express them in your own words.

   There may be times when it is appropriate to deviate from the study guide. For example, a question may have already been answered. If so, move on to the next question. Or someone may raise an important question not covered in the guide. Take time to discuss it, but try to keep the group from going off on tangents.

8. Avoid answering your own questions. An eager group quickly becomes passive and silent if members think the leader will do most of the talking. If necessary repeat or rephrase the question until it is clearly understood, or refer to the commentary woven into the guide to clarify the context or meaning.

9. Don't be afraid of silence in response to the discussion questions. People may need time to think about the question before formulating their answers.

10. Don't be content with just one answer. Ask, "What do the rest of you think?" or "Anything else?" until several people have given answers to the question.

11. Try to be affirming whenever possible. Affirm participation. Never reject an answer; if it is clearly off-base, ask, "Which verse led you to that conclusion?" or again, "What do the rest of you think?"

12. Don't expect every answer to be addressed to you, even though this will probably happen at first. As group members become more at ease, they will begin to truly interact with each other. This is one sign of healthy discussion.

13. Don't be afraid of controversy. It can be very stimulating. If you don't resolve an issue completely, don't be frustrated. Explain that the group will move on and God may enlighten all of you in later sessions.

14. Periodically summarize what the group has said about the passage. This helps to draw together the various ideas mentioned and gives continuity to the study. But don't preach.

15. Conclude your time together with the prayer suggestion at the end of the study, adapting it to your group's particular needs as appropriate. Ask for God's help in following through on the applications you've identified.

16. End on time.

Many more suggestions and helps for studying a passage or guiding discussion can be found in *How to Lead a LifeGuide Bible Study* and *The Big Book on Small Groups* (both from InterVarsity Press/USA).

Other InterVarsity Press Resources from N. T. Wright

The Challenge of Jesus
N. T. Wright offers clarity and a full accounting of the facts of the life and teachings of Jesus, revealing how the Son of God was also solidly planted in first-century Palestine. *978-0-8308-2200-3, 202 pages, hardcover*

The Challenge of Easter
The meaning of Easter seems lost among the colored eggs and chocolate candies. In this excerpt from *The Challenge of Jesus,* N. T. Wright explains Easter's bold, almost unbelievable claim: Jesus has risen from the dead. Here is God's announcement of an invitation to live as though God is among us, making everything new. *978-0-8308-3848-6, 64 pages, paperback*

Resurrection
This 50-minute DVD confronts the most startling claim of Christianity—that Jesus rose from the dead. Shot on location in Israel, Greece and England, N. T. Wright presents the political, historical and theological issues of Jesus' day and today regarding this claim. Wright brings clarity and insight to one of the most profound mysteries in human history. Study guide included. *978-0-8308-3435-8, DVD*

Evil and the Justice of God
N. T. Wright explores all aspects of evil and how it presents itself in society today. Fully grounded in the story of the Old and New Testaments, this presentation is provocative and hopeful; a fascinating analysis of and response to the fundamental question of evil and justice that faces believers. *978-0-8308-3398-6, 176 pages, hardcover*

Evil
Filmed in Israel, South Africa and England, this 50-minute DVD confronts some of the major "evil" issues of our time—from tsunamis to AIDS—and puts them under the biblical spotlight. N. T. Wright says there is a solution to the problem of evil, if only we have the honesty and courage to name it and understand it for what it is. Study guide included. *978-0-8308-3434-1, DVD*

Small Faith—Great God
N. T. Wright reminds us that what matters is not how much faith we have but Who our faith is in. Wright looks at the character of the faith God calls us to. He unfolds how dependence, humility and mystery all have a role to play. But the author doesn't ignore the messiness and difficulties of life, when hard times come and the unexpected knocks us down. He opens to us what faith means in times of trial and even in the face of death. Through it all he reminds us, it's not great faith we need: it is faith in a great God. *978-0-8308-3833-2, 176 pages, hardcover*

Justification: God's Plan and Paul's Vision
In this comprehensive account and defense of the crucial doctrine of justification, Wright also responds to critics who have challenged what has come to be called the New Perspective. Ultimately, he provides a chance for those in the middle of and on both sides of the debate to interact directly with his views and form their own conclusions. *978-0-8308-3863-9, 279 pages, hardcover*

Colossians and Philemon
In Colossians, Paul presents Christ as "the firstborn over all creation," and appeals to his readers to seek a maturity found only in Christ. In Philemon, Paul appeals to a fellow believer to receive a runaway slave in love and forgiveness. In this volume N. T. Wright offers comment on both of these important books. *978-0-8308-4242-1, 199 pages, paperback*